KEYS TO SUCCESSFUL BUSINESS PEAK:
Hidden business ethics on how to proceed to the best Business top

Leo Warren

Copyright
All rights reserved. No part of this publication may be reproduced, distributed or transmitted in any form or by any means, including photocopying, recording, or other electronic or mechanical methods without the prior written permission of the publisher, except in the case of brief quotations embodied in critical reviews and certain other non-commercial uses permitted by copyright law.

Copyright © Leo Warren, 2023

Table of content

Chapter 2	2
Chapter 3	2
Chapter 4	2
Chapter 5	2
Chapter 6	2
Chapter 7	2

Chapter 1 1

WHAT TRIGGERS AND TRIGGERED YOU?

BUDGETING

SPENDING PLAN TO ACCESS ORGANIZATION EXECUTION AS WELL AS BEING A SIGNIFICANT PIECE OF THE ARRANGING SYSTEM

WHAT DO YOU NEED ?

13 TIPS FOR EXPANDING YOUR BUSINESS AND THE GROWTH OF YOUR COMPANY

BEGINNING A BUSINESS REQUIRES SOMETHING OTHER THAN AN EXTRAORDINARY THOUGHT

HOW DO I MAKE USE OF MY PROFIT?

INTRODUCTION

Why Attitude will Represent the deciding moment in your Business and Why Having A Business Development Mentality Is the Most vital Phase in Your Prosperity.

Like most business visionaries, you need to develop your business.

On the off chance that you're simply beginning, you need to place yourself in a good position. In any case, whether you're new or have been attempting to construct your business for quite a while, one thing is without a doubt: you need development. What's more, you need it soon. All Its business visionaries' fantasy to be the following Steve Occupations, Imprint Zuckerberg, Elon Musk, or Jeff Bezos. Or on the other hand whoever their status is in your industry. You could have wandered into a business venture with a thought that you thought would be the following greatest thing. Yet, as you've most likely known at this point, extraordinary thoughts alone don't work. So you're stuck, as yet attempting to get your business going. You keep your business above water with the prospect that your constancy will get you someplace, some way or another. Presently, diligence pays off, but not consistently.

It could sound platitude, yet business achievement begins with the right attitude: the development outlook.
I bet you didn't think about how conceivable it is that you could be the one keeping your business down.
Without a business development outlook, that is the precise exact thing you're doing.
What is a Business Development Outlook?
Do you recall how, when you were more youthful, you were permeated with regular interest? Also, it was this feeling of miracle and investigation that filled your development and advancement into a grown-up. Yet, if you think back, you could see how you step by step different from a striking and inquisitive kid into one who's dependably careful about your current circumstance.

The majority of us are raised and educated into similarities with social qualities and assumptions. Tragically, this is added when we begin creating self-restricting predispositions and propensities about ourselves and the individuals around us. We figure out how to go with the crowd to acquire social acknowledgment. We become risk-unwilling because it is critical to our physical and social endurance. Set forth plainly, we foster the proper mentality.

A greater part of individuals has this outlook. They have a low capacity to bear the risk and have glaring misgivings of progress. As business visionaries, they're frequently:

Reluctant to leave their usual range of familiarity

Hesitant to fix something not broken

Like to leave things how they are as opposed to being faced with disappointment

However, this likewise implies passing up new open doors that could grow or try and open new entryways for business.

Interestingly, the development attitude is tied in with embracing change as a chance for development and learning. Individuals with a development mentality see expected even in each second. In business, this implies:

A receptiveness to better approaches for working

Facing challenges in the unexplored world

Building a culture of trial and error

Putting more accentuation on gaining from disappointment as opposed to dreading it

Assuming that you know Elon Musk's story, you'd realize that it hasn't forever been a series of wins for him. It's an account of fizzling and ascending from numerous disappointments.

Do you have a development outlook?

It's not difficult to be caught in a decent outlook when you're a business person.

After all, you need confirmation that you're continuously settling on the best choices. That is justifiable, however, it can likewise keep you from accomplishing development. Recognizing that there's an issue is the initial step to tracking down an answer. Now is the right time to pose yourself with the hard inquiries to learn if you're rehearsing a fixed or development outlook in your business.

1. Is your business serving your desired way of life?

You began your business because you needed to accomplish a specific way of life. Perhaps you maintained that more opportunities should acquire or work.

However, being good to go can truly challenge. On the off chance that you're feeling hopeless and worried constantly as opposed to carrying on with the way of life, you imagined, why do you remain?

2. What's your Enormous Why?

Knowing the solution to this can spell the distinction between you feeling energized or demotivated with your business.

For what reason did you get into this business? Did you simply get into it for the check?

As an expert, for example, I've found that motivation comes from the procuring potential as well as from the possibility of really having the option to help different business people. Indeed, we as a whole need to cover bills. Yet, as analysts would tell you, characteristic inspiration is more remarkable than outer wellsprings of inspiration. It's perfect to have the cash to take care of bills and accommodate my family, however, it likewise helps a great deal that I appreciate helping my clients and welcomes their concerns as new learning opens doors.

3. Could it be said that you are in the right business?

Some of the time individuals are in the right piece of the business, yet they're not in the right piece of the business. Or on the other hand, they're in some unacceptable business out and out.

That is completely fine. Nonetheless, you ought to likewise have the option to perceive when you're in some unacceptable spot and concede your slip-up.

This is where the significance of tolerating your mistakes and being available to groundbreaking thoughts comes in. Assuming you're reluctant to investigate the likelihood that you could be off-base about your items, clients, or plan of action, then you will not have the option to turn when important.

4. Is it true that you are infatuated with what you do or simply your thought?

Most thoughts look great when they're still in your mind or on paper.

It's another story when you begin carrying out them. That is the point at which the distinction between your assumptions and reality kicks in.

Regularly, having a smart thought doesn't ensure a decent business. Indeed, even Apple has its portion of bombed items.

Good thoughts with business potential don't in a split-second snap by the same token. Thoughts go through different emphases so it's by market needs.

5. Could it be said that you are accomplishing something you're enthusiastic about?

Can we just look at things objectively for a moment: business isn't continuously invigorating. It very well may be routine and boring.

So you want real interest in the thing you're doing. An energy that makes you love getting up ordinarily to do what you do. That will cause you to see the value in the intricacies of maintaining your own business as opposed to being disappointed by it.

This equivalent energy will make you endure even with hardships.

6. Is cash your main driver?

Cash is significant yet it ought not to be your main justification for needing to get into business. This takes us back to your "Huge Why," your driving reason in anything that you do.

Since your "Huge Why" will impact both little and major choices as a business visionary. It will decide the destiny of your business.

It is not necessarily the case that you ought to disregard the monetary parts of your business. It's an update that cash isn't the main benchmark for progress.

7. Could it be said that you are resolved to take the necessary steps?

Many individuals are wantrepreneurs. They need to become business people yet are reluctant to invest the effort to do it.

In truth, it isn't difficult to be a business person. Business visionaries need to There are no alternate routes to progress. It takes responsibility and a ton of penance to get a business going. The Bezos and Musks of the world put in a ton of sweat and tears before they got to where they are today.

All in all, do you have a fixed or a development outlook? On the off chance that you can sincerely answer indeed, then, at that point, great for you. If not, the following segment is for you.

Developing the Right Mentality for Business Development

As we've noted before, all people are brought into the world with a development outlook.

It fills our development and improvement when we're youthful. Be that as it may, this development outlook might be supported or smothered relying upon our encounters as we carry on with different life stages. Getting that development outlook back - or enhancing it - is tied in with stripping the layers of self-restricting convictions and predispositions that have turned into our default method of reasoning. To have the option to do this, we need to initially foster hesitance about our manners of thinking. Really at that time might we at any point work on our ways of behaving?

Clear the record for additional opportunities

To foster a development mentality, you want a new beginning.

You want to dispose of the stuff of the past so you can push ahead as a business person. This implies taking the examples from your encounters and afterward freeing yourself up to new ones. By taking a gander at the business visionary excursion as a fresh start, you can compose your example of overcoming adversity without any preparation. You can begin trusting in your capacities once more.

Allow yourself to come up short Disappointment is the greatest apprehension for some business people.

This dread deadens them and keeps them from making striking, high-influence choices. However, if you need to have a progress shot, you need to embrace disappointment as a piece of the excursion.

The best business people you know went through additional disappointments than you'll be aware. It was through the things they gained from flopping so often that they, at last, got better at what they do.

Stop flawlessness and loss of motion

Maintaining that everything should be perfect is ordinary. We would rather not settle for fair outcomes in our work.

But there are times when perfectionism can backfire. Some people, for instance, are paralyzed by waiting for the "perfect moment" to arrive. In business, this translates to waiting until you have the "perfect product" to launch, not realizing until it's too late that the chance to seize a great opportunity has already passed. Sometimes, you have to learn to settle with what's good enough so you can move your life and business forward.

Define your Big Why

The growth mindset is anchored on self-awareness and self-discovery.

To grow, you need to have a sense of purpose. This purpose is ultimately tied to your sense of identity as a person and as an entrepreneur.

Your Big Why clarifies what you want out of your business and your life serves as your rudder for steering closer to your entrepreneurial goals and aspirations.

Identify Your Profitable Zone of Genius

People not only have unique strengths, but they also have a Zone of Genius. These are the talents and skills that come naturally to you.

When you're doing something that's aligned with your Zone of Genius, you're able to effortlessly execute even the most challenging tasks.

Knowing your Zone of Genius is key to finding the line of business where you'll get the most fulfillment. That is the business where you can excel and satisfy your emotional needs at the same time.

Align Your Personal and Business Value Systems

Similar to your Big Why, your core values – the principles and ideals that you deem non-negotiable – are rudders that help you determine whether you're getting closer to or are going farther from your life goals.

That's why consistency between your personal and business value systems is important. Your business values need to reflect what you value as a person. Otherwise, you will unwittingly sow the seeds of self-doubt. The last thing you want is for your business values to come into conflict with what you hold dear as a person.

Be the Change that Your Business Needs

Anyone can be an entrepreneur, there's no license required to be one. But not everyone will be a successful entrepreneur. And now you know what sets the former apart from the latter: It's about the growth mindset.

The first key to your success as an entrepreneur is yourself. Your mindset boils down to: what do you want your business to do? Cultivating a growth mindset takes time and patience, but the rewards of doing so are well worth it.

Chapter 1

WHAT TRIGGERS AND TRIGGERED YOU ?

In business, a trigger is an event or an activity that causes a reaction or response. For example, an organization's business plan might incorporate a Trigger: In the event that a shopper spends a particular sum, they get a markdown on their resulting buy.

Promoting that utilizes time-explicit, designated messages or alerts is known as trigger showcasing. It is a method for making promoting more relevant to the individuals who view it. Each message to the purchaser in this strategy is achieved by a certain "occasion."

Basically, a deals trigger (otherwise called a buying trigger, a promoting trigger, or a change trigger) is any situation that can introduce a chance to reach out to a possibility. This will be an entirely different collaboration in certain conditions. In different cases, the trigger can incorporate reviving a lost open door.

A setting off occasion is a physical or theoretical hindrance or event that, when disregarded or met, triggers another occasion. Employment cutback, retirement, or passing are normal setting off occasions for different sorts of agreements.

The most vital phase in figuring out how to manage triggers is to know about the feelings you experience in light of something. Close to home triggers frequently emerge from the five detects, knowing about the things you feel, hear, smell, taste, and contact, as these could prompt a profound or conduct reaction.

A trigger is any improvement that you see to be distressing. It very well might be a particular individual, a subject you accept is dangerous, a power contrast, or a strange setting. At the end of the day, any of the circumstances above, and innumerable more, can be triggers.

Whatever drives you to begin a business shouldn't overwhelm you; a lot of want could lead you to begin a junky firm that returns little benefit, bringing about an enormous misfortune for you. Such an experience might make you lose revenue in bringing in cash; such an occurrence is a negative trigger.

One more illustration of a negative trigger is the point at which you start a business in light of the fact that a mate benefited from it, which might place you in an unfortunate circumstance inferable from your absence of complete comprehension and specialized expertise about the business. Subsequently, except if it is a squandered gamble, it is a generally excellent plan to have right comprehension prior to gambling.

Until you have a pay producing business outside your compensation, you may not be monetarily free. You will encounter genuine monetary achievement when you join otherworldly guidance with getting information. Get a positive trigger.

Chapter 2

BUDGETING

One of the most mind-blowing ways of spending cash is by planning. Fruitful independent ventures rely upon the viability of an entrepreneur's arranging cycle. One of the most basic components of the arranging system is business spending plan arranging, which is additionally one of the last phases of the arranging system. To start, you need to assemble organization monetary information, figures, and industry examination to assist you with building your business spending plan.

Alongside the monetary data and examination, in any case, you additionally need to remember the organization's overall business and brilliant courses of action to assemble your financial plan.

What Is a Business Spending plan?
A business spending plan is a dynamic, monetary arrangement used to gauge an organization's expected income and costs for an impending period. It is basically a monetary arrangement a business makes for a month, quarter, or year. It ought to be dynamic and adaptable so it very well may be changed as field-tested strategies and the market climate change

Business financial plans ought to incorporate each wellspring of income, or pay, expected by a firm alongside all potential consumptions the firm could make during a predefined period.

A nitty gritty and reasonable spending plan is one of the main devices for directing your business. A spending plan gives fundamental data to working inside your means, overseeing unforeseen difficulties, and making money. A legitimate financial plan will recognize accessible capital, gauge uses, and expected incomes. Entrepreneurs should ceaselessly allude to their spending plan as an approach to estimating gauge financial plan figures against genuine monetary outcomes to know where to adapt.

Arranging ought to represent long haul needs too. For instance, in the event that you expect an enormous use a couple of years not too far off for PC updates or gear upkeep, it's smart to begin planning ahead of time.

Business Financial plan Arranging Steps

A spending plan is a primary structure for your

business funds, itemizing past execution and giving a device to determine the financial year, or some other time, with a perspective on resources, income, and costs. Here is an outline of the monetary cycle:

Financial plan Readiness

Financial plans empower a business to precisely lay out objectives, needs, and spending covers, and detail where subsidizing starts and where new techniques could carry income into the organization cash safes. The details that order the most financing are high-need things like the wellsprings of income and the various sorts of costs. These things request exact accounting and act as execution signs of the general business technique.

A viable financial plan ought to separate income and expected costs by month, by quarter, or monetary year. Contingent upon the size of your business, it ought to incorporate separate spending plans for every division. These departmental spending plans ought to likewise be broken somewhere near month or by quarter, and aggregately, they will meet up to shape your lord financial plan.

The expert spending plan is an extensive monetary arrangement in light of the brilliant arrangement of the business firm. It is made out of two sub-spending plans — the working financial plan and the monetary financial plan. Each of these incorporates a lot more unambiguous spending plans.

Organizations that depend vigorously on occasional deals income act as a genuine illustration of why a financial plan is so significant. Having a methodology for circulating your income most really over a full financial year will assist with boosting benefits.

Chapter 3

SPENDING PLAN TO ACCESS ORGANIZATION EXECUTION

AS WELL AS BEING A SIGNIFICANT PIECE OF THE ARRANGING SYSTEM

Financial plans are important for assessing the exhibition of your organization over each monetary year. Normal sorts of planning in business are:

Static spending plans: Static financial plans are a kind of working spending plan that utilizes verifiable monetary information to financial plan for income and costs anticipated in the following period. Commonly utilized by tiny organizations, these financial plans require taking each detail and adding a rate increment or decline to it to mirror the following spending plan.

Execution based planning: This sort of financial plan considers the information sources and results per unit of item or administration to accomplish greatest proficiency.

Zero-based planning: A zero-based spending plan begins without any preparation like clockwork and fabricates another financial plan in view of the circumstances around then. At the end of the day, it begins from zero for each detail and uses interior and industry monetary information to fabricate the budget.

Fluctuation examination: A change based financial plan is one where genuine and expected values for each income and cost thing are determined. The outcomes are utilized to attempt to bring the spending plan things back inside a specific reach and accomplish improved efficiency The utilization of one of these sorts of organization spending plans can be one more apparatus for the monetary examination of the firm. For instance, assuming deals in the primary quarter are lower than what you planned, you'll be aware to track down costs to cut later in the financial year to remain productive. A more certain model may be deals of another item that surpasses assumptions. By following this pattern and contrasting it with what was planned, you will see that you have the extra income to maybe overhaul the spending plan with plans to build creation or recruit extra staff to deal with the additional business.

Spending plan to Get Supporting

A background marked by composing sound, definite spending plans and adhering to them can assist with showing banks or potential financial backers that you can foster a marketable strategy and make it work.

Moneylenders and financial backers need to dive profoundly into your funds and history. In the event that they don't see proof areas of strength for practices, it very well may be a warning that would dismiss them.

In the event that you're starting another business and have practically zero history, you really want to compensate for that absence of a history with definite help for your spending plan. This implies exploring the commercial center and showing how past patterns or, maybe a void in the business, upholds the numbers you present. This sort of meticulousness can assist you with acquiring serious thought from banks or financial backers.

Staffing for Planning

Indeed, independent companies with a couple of workers need to ensure they're staffed appropriately for composing and keeping a spending plan. If, for instance, you own and work a little bistro, you could have an interesting menu and a standing for quality client care, however that doesn't mean you're a monetary expert.

In the event that employing a full-time individual to deal with your spending plan and other monetary undertakings isn't sensible, consider temporary assistance or working with an outside counseling firm, particularly right off the bat and yearly when it comes time to compose another spending plan for the following financial year. SCORE, a business mentorship association subsidiary with the U.S. Private venture Organization (SBA), is made up to a great extent of workers with foundations in business and back who give direction and exhortation to independent ventures. This can be an important asset when you're simply getting everything rolling or when you're faced with a critical test. As well as assisting with planning or different issues, associations like SCORE can place you in contact with different assets locally.

Planning Programming

Probably the best instruments for composing a point by point financial plan and adhering to it are programming projects, and they go past Microsoft Succeed or other calculation sheet programs.

While searching for a planning programming program, you ordinarily need to search for these highlights:

Departmentalized planning: Enables you to make spending plans by office, division, or benefit focus and union them all into the expert financial plan.

Joint effort: Gives more than one individual in your association the capacity to chip away at the monetary arranging process.

Fluctuation correlation: Enables you to see real versus planned sums on a line-by-line basis.

Advantages of Business Spending plan: Arranging

In the event that a business doesn't foster a spending plan, it will confront a large group of issues. It is, really, stumbling along aimlessly on the off chance that it doesn't know how much income to expect or costs to want during a given time. Such a business will probably flop inside the initial two years after it opens.

The advantages of business spending plan arranging are a large number. Here are probably the most significant:

Monetary wellbeing: Without a business spending plan, you can't have the foggiest idea about the monetary soundness of your organization. You will have no clue assuming that you met or surpassed your objectives.

Vital preparation: A business spending plan permits you to foster a well thought out course of action since you will know the response to issues like whether you can grow.

Get obligation supporting: In the event that a private venture attempts to get obligation funding from a bank or other monetary establishment, it should create a spending plan to show possible moneylenders.

Draw in financial backers: to draw in financial backers in the business, those financial backers won't place their cash into the business except if they can see a spending plan.

Charge readiness: A business financial plan aids the arrangement of pay, deals, and finance charges.

Direction: To come to conclusions about any feature of the business, you need to know the amount of cash you possess at hand.

Chapter 4

WHAT DO YOU NEED ?

Numerous businesses wind up having their needs in Business

rather than that which is the need. Separating your business needs consists of seeing each business issue, goal, or circumstance, and the associated development of exercises expected to decide it. For example, if your business needs to manage client orders, you could observe the going with exercises: Get demands. Business needs are important entryways that are of fundamental importance to our affiliation. Right when an issue is knowledgeable about an affiliation, similar to a movement of client protests, a decrease in pay, or new market open entryways, we see business needs, all things considered.

    If someone asked you what your business needs today to make genuine progress tomorrow, how should you answer them? What data (and from where) might you guide for a reaction? It's a huge request since you truly need to really understand that your association ought to have the choice to keep a more viable business. The trouble notwithstanding, is that once in a while those necessities aren't exactly so particularly clear as they should be.

That is the place where some internal "digging" is required, yet it will in general be a mind-boggling task if you don't have the right gadgets. The inspiring news? Figuring out a smart method for keeping your business sound is direct with the right stage.

Describe your business objective

Separate your data and work processes

Examine revelations with your gathering

Make a Plan

Whether you're running your association on a clever development stage, coming up next are three phases you can take to perceive your business needs and make vital cycles to push it ahead:

1. Portray your business objective

A sensible business objective will be your North Star while perceiving your business needs and a way forward. Perhaps you have a guiding firm or an electronic office and your objective is to increase pay - that is great. To be reasonable notwithstanding, you'll need to get more granular than that. How might you want to build your pay? It could mean getting a better viewpoint on your advantage than recognize new pay channels or simply extending capability to help your return. What's vital for know is that you won't have an unquestionable reaction in regards to how you should approach achieving your objective until you plunge into specific data and gain some detectable quality into what's going on in your business.

2. Separate your data and work processes

While this is the normal ensuing stage in finding the arrangements you need, being the hardest part is by and large anticipated. Getting your hands on the data you need to seek after decisions with sureness is irksome when all that your work is scattered between different bookkeeping sheets and gadgets that don't talk with each other. Expecting get-togethers the right data to do this assessment sounds overpowering, you could have to contemplate different stages that can work on this. If you're in the advancing or design space and accept a phase ought to manage your errands, Mavenlink is a respectable decision since it permits you to follow time, expenses, and resources. On the other hand, if your association works in IT, Autotask combines your organization workspace, arrangements, exercises, and surging into one course of action. On the other hand, if you need a sagacious stage that will relate your gadgets overall and have to get an all out point of view on how capable and useful your business is, then, at that point, look at Accelo.

To put things into perspective, Brendon O'Sullivan, Head of Tremendous Blue Electronic, wound up in a relative boat. He knew he and his gathering were working harder than any time in ongoing memory however the numbers weren't adding up. While he endeavored to do some plunging into the association's financials, he comprehended there were a lot of weak sides concerning where people were effective money management their energy and how useful their endeavors were. That affirmation engaged him to see that his association was fighting a consequence of incapable gadgets and cycles, which were blocking their objective: growing pay. These pain points pushed him to place assets into more splendid development so he could get better detectable quality into his business.

3. Examine disclosures with your gathering

At the point when you're prepared to see this information and see your business "uncovered" (in the sum of its brightness) there's no covering what looks privileges easily. Presenting requests like: "how does my pay line up with how my gathering is working?" or "are there plans in how my gathering conveys or completes client work that consumes our essential concern?" won't be trying to answer. Brendon for instance, saw promptly that Immense Blue Electronic deferred charging process was hurting their pay, without a doubt.

Following placing assets into more splendid development, something Brendon had the choice to do was go from a 60-day receipt cycle to a 18-day receipt cycle (diminishing it by 70%). To perceive your business needs, you truly need to have a sensible business objective - Huge Blue digitals was to grow pay (and they did that by discarding inefficient cycles). In any case, you can't figure out how best to achieve your goal without speedily available and reliable data. You truly believe that detectable quality into your business should make more wise decisions and without a second thought push your association ahead.

4. Make a Game plan

Since you have a perception of your business targets, separated your data, and conferred the results to your gathering, the accompanying stage is to make a plan. While you're encouraging a once-over of critical advances your gathering ought to take, be reasonable, and be unequivocal.

Ponder what accomplishment suggests you to and check whether you can make a quantifiable and quantifiable objective to follow improvement. All in all, recall your objectives and assurance every task achieves the best outcomes.

This step will require some venture, but by putting careful thoughts into making a sensible game plan, you're extending the chances of ending up as the winner while decreasing the conceivable outcomes of disillusionment, disappointment, and an adjustment of plans. Making an aide is the best method for keeping your gathering on track and focused.

End

The means recorded above are vital to conclude your business needs and recognize new cycles that will drive the business toward progress. By tracking down a chance to achieve the fundamental work, you will really need to plan and remain focused in on achieving your business targets. Remember - this isn't a task you truly need to deal with alone. In case you're looking for a wise stage that can set you up for long stretch turn of events, look at Accelo. The primary objective is to help capable help firms manage their business undertakings immaculately.

Another point you should know is
Finance and comprehensive development
Finance is an imperative element for monetary development, yet there can likewise be a lot of it. This study examines what fifty years of information for OECD nations need to say regarding the job of the monetary area for financial development and pay disparity and draws strategy suggestions. Throughout the course of recent years, credit by banks and different go-betweens to families and organizations has grown multiple times as quick as monetary movement. In most OECD nations, further development is probably going to slow as opposed to support development. The organization of money matters for development. More credit to the confidential area eases back

development in most OECD nations, however more securities exchange supporting lifts development. Credit is a more grounded delay development when it goes to families as opposed to organizations. Monetary development fills more prominent pay imbalance in light of the fact that higher pay individuals can help more from the more noteworthy accessibility of credit and in light of the fact that the area pays high wages. Higher pay individuals can and do acquire more, so they can acquire more than others from the speculation that opens doors that distinguish.

The monetary area pays compensation which are above what representatives with comparable profiles acquire in the remainder of the economy. This premium is especially huge for top pay workers. There is no compromise between monetary change, development and pay correspondence in the long haul. For the time being, measures to try not to collect an excessive amount of credit can, nonetheless, limit development briefly. A solid commitment of the monetary area to comprehensive development requires solid capital supports, measures to decrease express and certain sponsorships to too enormous to-bomb monetary foundations and duty changes to advance impartiality among obligation and value funding.

3 WAYS TO IDENTIFY BUSINESS OPPORTUNITIES

With a foundational understanding of the types of opportunities that exist, you can dive into identifying them. Here are three ways you can do so and examples to learn from.

1. Identify Your Pain Points

When searching for potential market needs, start with yourself. In your everyday life, what processes or tasks bother you? What's the job to be done that you haven't quite found the perfect product to fulfill?

Many successful entrepreneurial ventures began with a personal problem in the founder's life. For instance, after Neil Blumenthal lost his prescription glasses and couldn't afford to buy new ones, he created an eyewear company that provides inexpensive, stylish glasses: Warby Parker.

Another example is the dating app Bumble, which Whitney Wolfe Herd created after leaving an abusive relationship. The app puts women first, requiring them to make the first move in heterosexual pairings, and advocates for gender equality and sexual harassment prevention.
Starting with personal questions can help determine if others have the same pain point and if opportunities are low-end or new-market disruptions.

2. Conduct Market Research
Another way to prove whether a business idea is viable is by conducting market research. This includes using industry research to define the competitive landscape and determine your target audience, as well as interviewing or surveying people who fit your target demographics.

Observing and gathering feedback from real people enables you to consider their perspectives and gain a deeper understanding of their motivations, frustrations, fears, and desires. This can help you conceptualize whether your product addresses a job to be done and the size of the audience that could benefit from it.

Once an opportunity is identified, you can utilize design thinking to create an innovative product that fits the job to be done you uncovered through research.

3. Question Processes

You can also identify business opportunities by examining the processes and delivery methods of existing product or service offerings. Try to evaluate each process with an open mind and ask questions about how you could improve it, such as:

Could this process be faster?

Could this process be executed using a cheaper business model?

Is there a more sustainable way to execute this process?

Does this process exclude certain groups of people? If so, is there a way to make the process accessible to all?

You don't have to reinvent the wheel to break into entrepreneurship—you just need to recognize the potential for innovation that already exists. When searching for business and market opportunities, you can identify customer needs that aren't being fulfilled, then assess them using his theory of disruptive innovation to determine if there's a low-end or new-market entry point for your product.

Rather than directly challenge companies dominating market segments, you can identify people who are over- or underserved by existing offerings and compete on a disruptive level.

To deepen your knowledge and learn how to craft an end-to-end disruptive strategy, consider taking an online course. Disruptive Strategy uses a "learn, practice, apply" approach: Christensen teaches key concepts and frameworks, then introduces case studies and interviews featuring real business leaders. Christensen also encourages you to put those frameworks on "like a set of lenses" and apply what you've learned to your business.

Are you interested in crafting an innovative strategy for your business? Explore our six-week course Disruptive Strategy, one of our online entrepreneurship and innovation courses. If you aren't sure which is the right fit, download our free course flowchart to determine which best aligns with your goals.

Chapter 5

13 TIPS FOR EXPANDING YOUR BUSINESS AND THE GROWTH OF YOUR COMPANY

This can be accelerated with these startup founders' advice, however there is no definite recipe for overnight success. Establishing your brand and starting to expand are your primary objectives when you first open your firm. Unfortunately, it takes time for this to happen. Hard work, perseverance, and dedication are necessary for growth, which is a continuous process. There is no specific action to do or method to employ in order to outperform other companies in the market or find quick success.

To achieve growth milestones that might propel a company to success, there are, however, tested methods.

1. *Make the right hires first.*

You must have a strong team to support you in achieving your goals before you can even consider your company's growth trajectory.

The only approach to guarantee rapid growth is to hire just the top candidates. "Having the appropriate team is everything."

Your business will be better prepared for future growth if you have diligent personnel who are committed to its success. Additionally, freeing up your time and energy to concentrate on critical work will enable you to perform at your best and foster a collaborative work environment.

2. *Pay attention to dependable money sources.*

Bill Reilly, a Wisconsin-based car repair entrepreneur, advised

focusing on the core consumers you already have rather than trying to gain new ones.
According to him, you may do this by putting in place a referral or customer loyalty program or by experimenting with marketing techniques based on past purchase patterns to promote repeat business.
If you're looking for investment, it's especially crucial that you concentrate on your existing market.
In the past, Reilly added, "we would emphasize our company's desire to become a franchise, which didn't resonate with banks. "We discovered that it's important to underline the scale of the market for what we do. A banker would be intrigued by this since they are more concerned with the return on investment than you are.

Expand your ongoing client base by carrying out a client unwaveringly program or evaluating promoting techniques in light of clients' buy narratives.

3. *Decrease your dangers*.
Risk is an unavoidable piece of beginning and growing a

business. It's difficult to control everything, except there are numerous ways of restricting inside and outside dangers to your organization and its development. One significant asset to assist you with achieving this is your business protection supplier.

"Private companies need to deal with their development to deflect interruptions that can carry business to a crushing end," said Mike DeHetre, VP of item improvement at Voyagers. For instance, "the burglary of worker information, client records, and item plans can obliterate an independent company, creating huge expenses and dissolving client certainty and reliability. Only one out of every odd entrepreneur's approach covers information breaks or other digital misfortunes. Private ventures ought to be ready by looking for protection items that assist them with recuperating, including those that cover the expense of remediation and claims."

As your private company develops, you might add space or

gear, make new items or administrations, or increment your working and circulation impression, so DeHetre prescribes intermittently evaluating your arrangement to guarantee you have the right inclusion.

"It's not difficult to fail to remember this step in the midst of quick extension, yet you would rather not figure out that you've grown out of your inclusion right when you really want it the most," he said.

4. Be versatile

One attribute that numerous effective new businesses share practically speaking is the capacity to change bearings rapidly in light of changes on the lookout. Lanng said that a lithe way to deal with advancement, both in your item and your organization, will assist you with developing all the more rapidly.

"By permitting yourself to adjust and change rapidly, you're ready to test various ways to deal with business and figure out what works best," Lanng told Business News Day to day. "It permits you to fizzle, pick yourself back up and continue onward." Chris Cornell, organizer, and Chief of Manhead Product said his organization has viewed flexibility as key in extending its client base past its underlying spotlight on music stock.

"Shift focus over to current mainstream society patterns for an amazing chance to turn out to be important for the development when it checks out," he said. "In a time of web popularity, we hoped to extend our points of view past the music business. We collaborated with 'The Ruler of Mainstream society' and Insta-popular little guy, Doug the Pug, to deliver his new stuff. Perceiving the compass and notoriety of Doug, we had the option to take his product to a higher level, expanding our plan of action past groups."

5. Center around your client experience.

Clients' discernments can represent the deciding moment of your business. Convey quality encounters and items, and they'll rapidly praise you enthusiastically via web-based entertainment; wreck it, and they'll tell the world significantly quicker. Quick development relies upon fulfilling your current and possible clients with their experience.

"Contrasted and enormous organizations, private ventures are deft and frequently better ready to see, expect, and answer their client's necessities," DeHetre said. "The best independent ventures exploit this benefit by offering new and imaginative items and administrations for sale to the public all the more rapidly and creating and supporting long haul client connections."

Dennis Tanjeloff, president and Chief of Astro Display of Pearls, concurred. He expressed paying attention to your clients and giving them what they need is of most extreme significance.

[Learn how client relationships with the board programming can assist you with better comprehension of your customers.]

"Differentiate your contributions so you can best take care of the clients' evolving tastes," Tanjeloff said. "Keep in mind, you are here to serve the client - it's the reason you are just getting started."

While drawing in with your crowd is vital, customizing the experience can help and reinforce that relationship.

6. *Put resources into yourself*

In the beginning phases of your business, you'll probably see an extremely lean net revenue (or no benefit by any means), so any cash you truly do make ought to go straightforwardly to assisting you with developing.

"A startup's capacity to put resources into itself [helps] speed up development," Lanng said. "In those early years, it's basic to ensure that you're diverting any income back into the organization. It's crucial to contribute early and intensely to rapidly develop."

While it may very well be enticing to take every one of your benefits, it's smarter to put resources into your business' development so you can receive greater rewards later. Figure out what parts of your business need more consideration: For instance, do you have to recruit more specialists, grow your advertising endeavors, or secure extra financing? At the point when you track down an essential region that needs improvement, give that region your monetary help.

7. *Continuously think ahead*

While deftness is a significant quality for a startup, you can't take a blind leap of faith while you're maintaining a business. Arranging your subsequent stage - fully expecting every conceivable situation - is the most ideal way to remain grounded and secure as your business develops.

Thinking ahead is expansive counsel, yet it very well may be basically as straightforward as looking into every single continuous agreement, such as contrasting rates and the best charge card processors and checking whether you can arrange a more ideal arrangement.

8. *Support your client assistance*

One more extraordinary technique for developing your business is to zero in on giving unrivaled client assistance. At the point when you surpass clients' assumptions, they are probably going to tell their companions, family, and adherents about your business.

At the point when you exceed all expectations, for example, by offering limits in the event that a client has an unfortunate encounter or following up to guarantee a client was happy with your item or administration, you lay out a standing for extraordinary client support. [Make sure you have the best business telephone framework for your client care team.]

9. Center around web-based entertainment

One more technique to develop your business is to make profiles on every one of the significant virtual entertainment stages (Instagram, Facebook, Twitter, and so forth.). A functioning profile permits you to all the more likely market your business and interface with undeniably more possible clients.

At the point when your business has a record that you update consistently on significant stages, customers can find your business all the more effectively and are bound to impart your business to their companions. You'll likewise make a really captivating encounter for your crowd, assisting them with feeling more associated with your image and developing trust.

10. Go to systems administration occasions

Organizing occasions permit you to associate with similar people, large numbers of whom have extraordinary viewpoints and bits of knowledge that can assist you with developing your business. The associations and connections that come from going to systems administration occasions can be advantageous long into the future.

11. Practice corporate social obligation

Shoppers need to purchase from organizations energetic about causes that assist with making the world a superior spot. Whether you give to malignant growth exploration or backing a not-for-profit, for example, a destitute sanctuary, search for ways of contributing seriously to the causes you are backing and offer that with your clients. You could openly communicate your help to underserved networks, give to different associations, offer your opportunity to pledge drives, and deal feasible items to help the climate. There are numerous ways of being socially dependable as a business; track down not many that work for you.

12. Have nearby occasions

While going to occasions is an incredible method for developing your organization, facilitating your occasions inside your local area is considerably more useful - whether it's running a pledge drive, offering select arrangements on a vacation, or supporting a neighborhood sports group. Making a novel encounter for your clients will cultivate more private associations with them.

Assuming you have occasions in your space, you'll increase brand mindfulness and show your local area that you are putting resources into their prosperity. At the point when you are focused on them, they'll feel more dependability to your business.

13. Research your rivals

While this probably won't evoke quick development, exploring your rivals is perhaps the main initial phase in sending off your business. Ask yourself who your rivals are, what they're doing (that you're not doing) that works for them, and how you can separate your business from theirs. The responses to these inquiries will assist you with framing a more useful business methodology, characterizing the region of your business that require more thoughtfulness regarding prospering

Chapter 6

BEGINNING A BUSINESS REQUIRES SOMETHING OTHER THAN AN EXTRAORDINARY THOUGHT

To win in business today, you ought to be versatile and have extraordinary planning and definitive capacities. Numerous people start a business envisioning that they'll turn on their laptops or open their doorways and start getting cash, just to see that acquiring cash in a business is fundamentally surprisingly problematic.

You can avoid this in your endeavors by taking as much time as the need should arise and organizing out all of the fundamental advances you need to gain ground. Anything kind of business you want to start, using the going with nine clues can help you with making progress in your undertaking.

KEY Significant focuses:
Starting a business requires logical thinking, chose affiliation, and organized record-keeping.

It's fundamental for have some familiarity with your resistance and either appropriate or refine their productive systems.

You'll for certain end up turning out more persistently for yourself than you would for someone else, so plan to make repentances in your own life while spreading out your business.

Offering incredible help to your clients is crucial to procuring their faithfulness and holding their business. Guarantee not simply that the business is ready for ship off, but you are as well.

9 useful Ways of growing A Productive Business

1. Get Composed

To gain the business headway you ought to be composed. It will help you with completing liabilities and keep consistent over things to do. A compelling strategy for being composed is to make an arrangement for the day consistently. As you complete everything, mark it off your overview. This will ensure that you're not neglecting to recollect that anything and completely finishing all of the positions that are essential for the perseverance of your business.

2. Keep Organized Records

All productive associations keep point by point records. In this way, you'll know where the business stands fiscally and what potential troubles you could defy. Essentially knowing this offers you a chance to think of methodology to vanquish those troubles.

Most associations are choosing to keep two courses of action of records: one physical and one in the cloud. By having records that are constantly moved and upheld, a business never again needs to worry about losing its data. The genuine record exists as a support yet, when in doubt, it is used to ensure that different information is correct.

3. Separate Your Resistance

Competition breeds the best results. To make genuine

progress, you can't be hesitant to study and acquire from your adversaries. In light of everything, they may be achieving something right that you can execute in your business to get more income. How you examine competition will change between regions. If you're a diner owner, you may simply have the choice to eat at your resistance's bistros, ask various clients what they think, and gain information that way. Nevertheless, you could be an association with significantly more limited induction to your opponents, similar to a manufactured association. In light of everything, you would work with a business master and clerk to go over not precisely what the business presents to the world, yet any financial information you could have the choice to get on the association as well.

4. Handle the Risks and Prizes

The best approach to making progress is continuing with

possibly perilous strategies to help your business with creating. A fair request to present is "What's the disservice?" If you can answer this request, then, you comprehend what the most terrible circumstance possible is. This data will allow you to take such possibly risky approaches that can make colossal awards.

Understanding risks and prizes consolidate being clever about the preparation of starting your business.

5. Be Innovative

Constantly be looking for approaches to dealing with your business and make it stand separated from the resistance. See that you don't know everything and be accessible to pivotal contemplations and different ways of managing your business.

6. Stay on target

The notable maxim "Rome wasn't intrinsic a day" applies here. Since you open a business doesn't mean you will expeditiously start getting cash. It expects speculation to let people know your personality, so focus on achieving your transient targets.

Various business visionaries don't for even a second see an advantage for two or three years while they use their earnings to recuperate adventure costs. This is classified "losing money hand over fist." When you are helpful and make an overabundance to spend to cover commitments and money, this is called being "working at a benefit."

That being said, in case the business isn't bringing in cash after a critical period, it justifies researching if there are issues with the thing or organization if the market really exists, and other potential issues that could slow or stop a business' turn of events.

7. Plan to Make Repentances

The lead-up to starting a business is troublesome work, yet after you open your entrances, your work has as of late begun. You, taking everything into account, need to contribute more energy than you would expecting that you were working for someone else, which could mean money management less time with friends and family to make progress.

The precept that there are no closures of the week and no journeys for business people could sound substantial for the people who are centered around making their business work. Nothing terrible can be said about standard work, and a few business visionaries misconceive the certified cost of the compensations that are supposed to start and keep a useful business.

8. Offer Uncommon Help

Various productive associations neglect to recollect that giving phenomenal client help is critical. Accepting you offer better help for your clients, they'll be more arranged to come to you the accompanying time they need something rather than going to your resistance.

In the present hyper-relentless business environment, regularly the isolating variable making genuine progress and unprofitable associations is the level of organization that the business gives. This is where the maxim "undersell and surpass assumptions" comes being utilized, and smart business people ought to truly follow it.

9. Be Consistent

Consistency is a fundamental part to getting cash in business. You really want to keep on doing what is essential to make genuine progress all week long. This will make long stretch positive affinities that will help you with getting cash over an extended time.

What Is the Fastest Way for a Business to Create?

Associations will create at their rates, and normally this is out of the control of the business person or workers. Regardless, a couple of parts of running lean could help a business with growing quickly, for instance, focusing in on a little item offering, expanding rather than scaling back, and giving a prominent edge over your opponents or some likeness thereof.

How Might You Grow Arrangements?

Growing arrangements can arise out of maybe a couple of spots. You can increase publicizing utilizations where it has a shown effect, offer references from existing clients, manufacture a direct-to-client email once-over, and others. You can moreover grow an item offering, yet if it neglects to measure up to assumptions, it will unfavorably impact your primary concern.

What Makes a Startup Productive?

Business accomplishment is a problematic plan to quantify anyway if it suggests delivering returns for accomplices, new organizations can be an incredible strategy for conveying returns. The best new organizations have a fair thing or organization that is flexible. The startup can turn quickly, sort out the market and its financial situation, and is ready to take full advantage of chances when they present themselves.

Chapter 7

HOW DO I MAKE USE OF MY PROFIT?

Benefits of 5 Private Company Activities. It's wonderful that your business is doing well and that you are making money. How to manage the benefits of your independent firm is the question at hand.

Private enterprise Advantages
Many business owners experience challenging moments in the early stages when they are constantly questioning whether their private enterprise will ever be profitable. When starting a business, one of the main goals is for it to take off and become productive to the point where you understand it will be profitable for as long as feasible. If your own business is currently profitable, congratulations. That is a tremendous accomplishment for your company, and your tenacious work is finally bearing fruit!

Business means that complacency is never an option, of course. The next business decision to make is how to use the benefits once your firm is profitable. If your business is still in its early stages, paying yourself more is related to positioning it for long-term success and future growth rather than merely buying yourself something nice.

Here are five wise decisions that business owners should take into account when deciding how to use their perks.

What You Need to Know About the Benefits of Independent Business

We should take a minute to define benefits and explain how to quantify them before moving on to how to use benefits. Experts advise all businesspeople to learn how to order and use a profit and loss statement (P&L). If all else fails with regard to any of your P&L statistics, it's best to err on the side of caution so that you don't overcommit to plans or activities that your company is ill-equipped to handle.

P&L explanations satisfy a range of purposes. First of all, they provide you with a fair indication of your company's continued financial viability. Second, they enable you to project future business profits and create financial strategies. Finally, your P&L will help you determine your net total revenue. In simple words, your organization's productivity may be summarized by looking at your net total revenue.

Benefits of 5 Private Company Activities

It's wonderful that your business is doing well and that you are making money. How to manage the benefits of your independent firm is the question at hand.

Private enterprise Advantages Many business owners experience challenging moments in the early stages when they are constantly questioning whether their private enterprise will ever be profitable. When starting a business, one of the main goals is for it to take off and become productive to the point where you understand it will be profitable for as long as feasible. If your own business is currently profitable, congratulations. That is a tremendous accomplishment for your company, and your tenacious work is finally bearing fruit!

Business means that complacency is never an option, of course. The next business decision to make is how to use the benefits once your firm is profitable. If your business is still in its early stages, paying yourself more is related to positioning it for long-term success and future growth rather than merely buying yourself something nice.

Here are five wise decisions that business owners should take into account when deciding how to use their perks.

What You Need to Know About the Benefits of Independent Business

We should take a minute to define benefits and explain how to quantify them before moving on to how to use benefits. Experts advise all businesspeople to learn how to order and use a profit and loss statement (P&L). If all else fails with regard to any of your P&L statistics, it's best to err on the side of caution so that you don't overcommit to plans or activities that your company is ill-equipped to handle.

P&L explanations satisfy a range of purposes. First of all, they provide you with a fair indication of your company's continued financial viability. Second, they enable you to project future business profits and create financial strategies. Finally, your P&L will help you determine your net total revenue. In simple words, your organization's productivity may be summarized by looking at your net total revenue.

1. Keep for Later

Your reserve money is one of the most important things to take into account as you start to reap the benefits. Do you have a sufficient rainy day asset to support your operating capital needs if a crisis expense or unexpected revenue halt were to occur?

Look at the costs of maintaining your firm for more than a month. Investigate your bank balance after that. How long could the lights be kept on if there was a significant drop in revenue or a significant increase in expenses? How long could you eventually be able to keep paying your merchants and representatives? In the event that you encounter a challenging scenario, think about keeping enough cash on hand to guarantee you can cover your working capital for a considerable amount of time.

That is a fantastic way to ensure the longevity of your company even during a downturn. Additionally, it increases the organization's value, which might be beneficial if you're looking for financial supporters or, alternatively, want to sell your ownership interest to meet your personal financial needs.

2. Employ Business Advantages to Grow Your Business

It is crucial to run all the figures and consult your consultants before attempting to use benefits for business expansion or development. It would be beneficial to go back to your plan right now.

You need to determine whether reinvesting your current benefits and incurring more expenditures will be sufficient in the long run. Development plans should only be initiated if it is clear that your company can afford the additional operating costs.

If you decide to keep using the profits from your independent enterprise to expand your firm, you have a number of options:

Perhaps you need to spend more money on marketing to expand your clientele.

Or, on the other hand, if you already have a thriving, expanding clientele, perhaps this is the perfect moment to start new lines of business so you can upsell to current customers or attract new ones.

In order to service more clients, you also have the option of hiring extra help.

If your physical firm would benefit from a longer lasting image, you might be able to expand your location or relocate. Also keep in mind that you might not always need to have extra cash on hand to pay for additional space, equipment, or faculty. You can decide that you want to use the assistance to help you pay for those necessities.

3. Reduce or renegotiate the debt

It's possible that you made it necessary for you to start your business. If this was your most memorable project, you could have been required to obtain funding at a rather high cost.Therefore, you might want to think about renegotiating and applying some of your benefits to paying off debt.

You have two main options here: either you may make sizable payments against the principal balance of your debt or you can try to renegotiate. You could need to provide your updated financial information to lenders to explore renegotiating if your credit has an excessive loan cost. If you can demonstrate that your company is profitable, you may be able to renegotiate your loan terms at a reduced interest rate because your risk of default is decreased.

If you pay off the head, you'll pay less interest throughout the course of the advance, which will save you money.

4. Use Business Advantages to Pay Yourself

Finally, another technique for using your business benefits is to pay yourself, the business person. The use of business benefits for owner compensation rates can be to some degree tangled, dependent upon the legitimate plan of your movement. Coming up next are several fundamentals to consider.

If your association is a sole proprietorship or another pass-through component, all of your advantage streams straightforwardly to you as pay in any event. If you're running a C Corp, you can pay yourself a pay. If you start to see benefits, you by and large have the decision to pay yourself and furthermore your agents more. Recall that you would prefer not to subvert your future growth opportunities, so raises should be reasonable. Besides, if you're locked in with an association or a business with various owners, you'll all need to agree (or get a bigger vote, typically) in regards to a few answers for advantages and pay.

Before you decide to pull the advantages out as a pay, try to talk with your cost guide. If your compensation would be charged at a higher rate than your business' compensation, you would have to remain with your remuneration and let the value of your association increase. On the other hand, paying you an enormous pay could moreover reduce the association's obligation. That all depends upon the specific numbers included, so you'll need to see a specialist.

As well as paying yourself a remuneration or prize, you could have to ponder conveying yourself a benefit. A "benefit" is a portion made to financial backers in a C Corp. There are many possible proposition plans, yet in the most clear one (where there's simply a solitary kind of deal), everyone gets a benefit comparable with their ownership. You don't have to pay all of your advantages out thusly; you can pick any aggregate per share. The association can't limit benefits, meaning it pays a charge on that total, but your cost rate on benefits is basically 15%. Yet again whether or not this is shrewd depends upon the practical cost rates for your business and yourself, so you'll need to banter with an obligation counsel.

5. The total of the Previously mentioned

Clearly, you don't have to show up to win big or bust decisions about how to deal with your cash once your association shows up at the dim. You could choose to give cash in the association to fabricate its worth, convey a benefit, and moreover give your laborers raises. You could buy one more piece of equipment and add your pay. It truly relies upon you and your goals for keeping up with your business. Being uninformed basically infers you have altogether more choices and important entryways!

No matter what your point of view could appear to be good with respect to using your advantages, you should continually guide an obligation capable. Remember that accepting at least for a moment that you're running a pass-through substance, you'll have to pay charge on your advantages at your rate. Moreover, if you're running a C Corp, your business ought to pay a charge for those advantages. Banter with your cost counsel about your business targets and money related situation; they'll have the choice to help you with figuring your net effective obligation rate (ensuing to applying all of the possible inductions, suspensions, workarounds, and segments) and work out a course of action that supports both your obligation capability and your objectives.

www.ingramcontent.com/pod-product-compliance
Lightning Source LLC
Chambersburg PA
CBHW071145240526
45465CB00024BA/1778